Life is Not Fair, and Life is Not Kind, Life is an Opportunity

By Albert L. Swope

Copyright

© Copyright 2019 Albert L. Swope

All Rights Reserved.

ISBN: 9781081311827

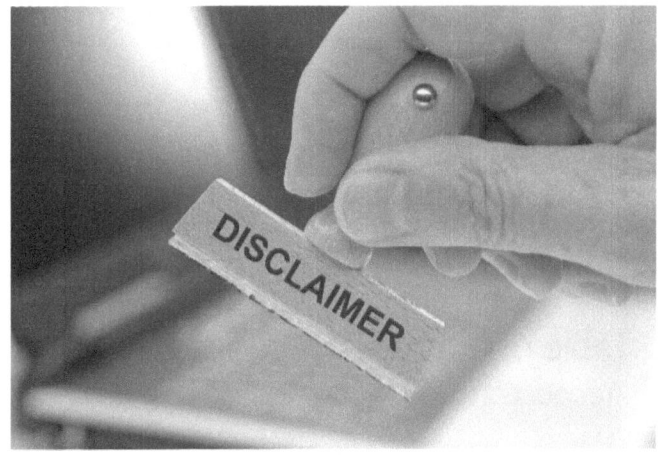

Disclaimer

No warranty whatsoever is being expressed or implied regarding the contents of this book.

Albert l Swope

Table of Contents

Introduction 1

Life is Not Fair 4

   Tips for Stopping Your Thought Process 6

   Final Practice Tips 8

Life is Not Kind 10

   Coping with Unkind Behavior 14

Grabbing Opportunities 15

   Steps to Building Confidence 17

      Seeking Opportunities................... 18

Final Tips 20

Conclusion 22

Albert l Swope

Life Is An Opportunity

*Life is. Not life should be, or I wish life was,
Life happens, just because.
A wolf preys on a weakened elk, not because it prefers the taste,
But rather it is nature's way to end the elk's fate.*

*The elk provides nourishment for the wolf clan,
This is natural, it is life's plan.*

*No vote is taken in the pack,
To determine the best plan of attack.*

*The wolves know in order to survive,
Acting on opportunity will help them thrive.
Indecisiveness would result in failure,
And failure leads to death.*

*If you are looking for fairness in nature, it will not be found.
If you are looking for kindness, stop looking around.
If you are waiting for opportunity to present itself to you,
It will pass you by, and then you're through.*

*Look for opportunity and act without hesitation.
Seize opportunity it is the means to an end.
Life is opportunity, no room for rivals.
Embrace opportunity, for it is survival.*

-- Albert L. Swope

Introduction

Success comes to the prepared, the willing, and to those who are able to do what is required to succeed.

Machiavelli did not look upon human nature with any kindness. He felt human nature was unreliable and motivated by self-interest. During his time of princes, kings, and other rules, Machiavelli felt people would change rules as a way to improve their life. He felt they were irrational and incapable of knowing what would be best. Machiavelli had plenty of examples of hypocrisy, which showed naïve, unwary, and vapid rulers.

Discussing that life is not fair or kind, but an opportunity, it seems that Machiavelli had something correct. The success and happiness one finds in life are more about Machiavellian survival of the fittest. It is about who is the strongest, who is willing to work the hardest, and who is willing to be unkind and not complain about "unfairness."

There are certainly plenty of political philosophies espousing otherwise, and perhaps they work when one considers the throes of death. Even a wild animal will cry out, whether it is crying about how unfair it is to die or just because of the pain they suffer before the end, it is difficult to say.

But, if you are going to succeed, you have to quit looking for the opportunity to be given to you. You must stop looking for "fairness" in life and do what is required. Life is a competition, especially among animals in the wilderness, so why would you think otherwise? We are supposedly "advanced intelligent creatures," but let's face it, at the end of the day, it is still the survival of the fittest, the one that gets there first, and the one that makes enough noise and effort that is recognized.

If you think life is fair or kind, and that things should just be handed to you, then you do so at your own peril.

Life's opportunities only arrive when you grab them by the short-hair and do not let go. This guide is not about letting go of your morals, your ethics, or telling you to commit illegal acts as a way of making life better. It is about grabbing the opportunities you have at your fingertips and ensuring your conscience is clear as you work hard to achieve what you can—not what you "deserve" because you were born, but what you can achieve because of your own hard work, intelligence, and desire.

You are going to learn how to move past the whining and discover success, as you continue.

Life is Not Fair

"First and foremost, life is about competition, so, brace the fact and do what must be done."

-- Albert L Swope

Life is not fair. History and the wild animal kingdom show us this on a regular basis. The little bunny that didn't hop fast enough is eaten by the coyote. It is the cycle of nature. To think that you won't be swallowed up or miss opportunities while waiting for them to come to you—is wrong.

Here is an example of someone who sat back and did not take opportunities.

The person married for love despite knowing the spouse was just like the parent, always spending too much and out for number one. Through marriage, the person was never able to own a home, save money, and live a steady, comfortable life. It is easy to blame the spouse, and there is plenty of wrongs done by this spouse. However, the control was given to the spouse. The person did not try to make life better in all senses of the word and instead kept compounding the problem by letting the unhappiness reign. Now even after a divorce, unhappiness continues because the pattern is established—the control is always in the ex-spouse's hand—never in the person's hand.

If you allow others to control you, to take any opportunity before you, and still complain you will "never have anything you want," then you are looking at the situation in the negative and not looking for the way to make things happen to benefit you.

Tips for Stopping Your Thought Process

You need to redirect your thoughts. You need to change how you perceive life before you can take the opportunities presented to you. For those who always think life should be handed to them that they were born deserving, it is going to be hard to make changes and realize that life is not fair. However, if you have finally come to the realization that things are not going the way you want and you have not put in the effort, then you are ready for the tips.

- ✓ Use journaling or self-talk to air your grievances.

- ✓ Using the same methods begin to assess your life from a distinct perspective. What would someone say to you who might have less than you? What would a successful person say to you?

- ✓ Write or think about five things you can change about how you perceive life.

It is going to take time to change your mindset. Just knowing that life is not fair after you have had a lifetime of thinking it should be, is not going to change overnight. You are also going to have difficulty changing your perspective, but it must be done.

When it is tough, and you feel you have tried to take this opportunity of changing your mindset without avail, you may need to seek a psychologist or therapist who can offer you a varied perspective. Sometimes gaining outside help, from someone who is not familiar with you, can help you to be called on the behaviors you continue to follow and the patterns of blaming others or thinking that others have more.

The irony is that we often think someone else has a better life, and until you analyze what they do not show you; you don't know how great you might have it.

The statement "until you have walked a mile in another's shoe" is apt here. We all like to think that others have it better or forget that others might have it worse.

Final Practice Tips
To help change your mindset further and to gain the unbiased perspective, accepting that life is not fair, you need one more tip.

- ✓ Each day finds someone who has a worse life and considers how you would be living in their shoes.

For example, let's say the person who married wrong is suddenly facing charges for something they didn't do. The pattern is clear, and when presented the person is exonerated, but life being unfair ensured that it took over three years for the pattern to present itself in such a way for the false charges to turn into malicious intent conducted by the spouse.

What would you do in that situation? Would your normal life, where you go out with friends, can afford the bills, and your steady job, without that promotion be enough to satisfy you?

Let's use another example. This time it is a person who survived a bombing but lost their legs. Life was pretty normal, until running in a race where bombs went off, and now, life is changed forever. It wasn't fair to be in the exact place that the majority of the blast was, but it happened.

These examples may be extreme, but they are also designed to bring about a new thought process. If you can empathize and think "I could have it worse," then the fact that life is not fair for anyone, even you, will stop bothering you and you can move on to the next discovery—life is not kind—either.

Life is Not Kind

"There was no such thing as a fair fight. All vulnerabilities must be exploited."

— *Cary Caffrey*

Fairness, with innocent until proven guilty, and equality in the workplace doesn't exist because of human nature rules. People are biased. They are out for themselves and darn the consequences. Worse, if those who deeply commit improper acts keep getting away with things, they continue. Someone will always think they know what is "best" for everyone else. Someone will always be out for themselves regardless of who it hurts.

It would be wonderful if we could all believe in the Buddhist precepts, which are quite similar to most religions, just without the negativity and the guilty.

There are the moral precepts Buddhists believe in, and four are listed here:

- ✓ I will care for all living things, including the smallest organisms.
- ✓ I will take only what is given to me.
- ✓ I will observe true speech.
- ✓ I will abstain from intoxicants.

Now think about Catholicism for a moment.

- ✓ I shall not kill.
- ✓ I shall not commit adultery.
- ✓ I shall not lie.
- ✓ I shall not steal.

Notice "not" is in each phase of the four examples from Catholicism, while the Buddhists use positive speech. What you believe in with regards to religion is up to you, but the example of positive thinking versus

Albert l Swope

negative thinking is helpful in moving on from life not being fair or kind.

The example of a Buddhist way of life, where kindness is first nature and not second is what your focus should be on rather than the negative.

What if every person truly approached another with kindness and empathy, instead of self-gain and self-reward? We wouldn't have war; we would have peace, acceptance of differences from races to religion.

Unfortunately, life is made up of biases, anger, and plenty of negative emotions, with narcissism as a key factor.

We like to pretend that we would be kind to others and listen to them, but how often do you talk about yourself? When you ask someone else how they are doing, and they do not provide a detailed description, do you let it go and talk about yourself again? Until you can move on from being unkind to others and accept that others will continuously be unkind, you are not going to be able to take the opportunities that exist.

Let's provide an example. A person works with someone who has been in the same industry part-time for 20 years. The older person is passive-aggressive forcing, the newer person to make decisions when kindness is to defer to the one who has more longivity. The newer person was leaving some work for the other person to do because the newer person had already done quite a bit having arrived at work for the morning shift. The boss stated, "that is kind of you, but person B already has enough, so go ahead and get this done." On any other day, the passive-aggressive attitude would have taken the boxes, opened everything, and done it all without sharing the workload despite having told the newer person that each step should be shared.

When you look at that example, what would you do? Would you take all the work for yourself or try to be kind and fair, and share?

Have you had enough of people being unkind that you would rather step on toes, go against your morals, and just take and keep taking?

Think about these questions and the example.

Coping with Unkind Behavior

To take an opportunity does not mean, you should be unkind. You can retain your soul, and in fact, it is a challenge to you to keep your kindness and sense of fairness, while you gain new opportunities.

Life may be unkind, and so are people, but that does not mean you have to wallow in it. You can stand up and be strong.

- ✓ Start with empathy again. Think of examples where life has been unfair and unkind to others, and how would you respond?
- ✓ Write these things down or just meditate on them.
- ✓ Think about when someone stepped all over you to rise to a new position in work or betrayed you. How did you react, and how would you do things differently?
- ✓ List ways you can deal with how unkind life is.

Put these ways into action.

Grabbing Opportunities

"Most of the important things in the world have been accomplished by people who have kept on trying when there seemed to be no help at all."

– Dale Carnegie

The above sections have tips and exercises to help you come to terms with how unfair and unkind life will always be, no matter who you are. Until you have come to a place in your mind, where you feel comfortable with your current life, you are not ready to grab opportunities that come along. But that doesn't mean you should sit back and let them pass you by either. There are exercises you can do to prepare yourself for the opportunities that are going to appear.

For example, a person was in her late fifties when her husband was diagnosed with dementia. During childhood, her mother told her she was stupid, and all she was good for was being a hairdresser. Since her childhood, this mother of two became a contractor, with a general contractor's license, worked as a bookstore manager, and when her husband became ill—she earned her Medical Assistant and Certified Nursing Assistant certifications.

Life is not over even if you are getting older, that is lesson one. You can always become someone new, someone, you can love more than you have in the past.

Steps to Building Confidence
Part of the problem is confidence. You might think you have confidence, but when you get in the trap of feeling that life is unfair and

unkind just to you or your close family and friends, you do not have confidence.

You need to build it back up.

- ✓ Use journaling to write about hardships and positive aspects.

- ✓ Use the journal to list one excellent quality you have each day. (You can also do this in your head, whatever works for you)

- ✓ Take a small step toward something you desire. For example, a writer might publish a book online under a pseudonym to get the confidence to send query letters to the big five publishers.

- ✓ Build your confidence for the hobby, job, or what you want by continuing to work on strengthening your knowledge. If you want a promotion, then get more education, speak with your manager about what you can do to fit the role in a year or two. Talking shows your interest, and also helps build your confidence because you are doing something to prepare what you want to gain.

Seeking Opportunities

Once you have confidence, you need to seek more opportunities for what you want in life. You will have to buck human nature, biases, unkind behavior, and unfairness. But you can seek opportunities.

From a work perspective:

- ✓ Gain knowledge
- ✓ Get more educational certifications
- ✓ Speak with management about new steps
- ✓ Ask why you did not get the promotion, what can you do better, what does management want to see from you?
- ✓ If you still get the feeling of biased behavior, apply to other places.
- ✓ Change jobs and give a new company a chance to see your potential.
- ✓ Use your confidence to show that you want to pursue more than you already have.

From a life perspective – Relationships:

Do you want your relationships to improve? We all do, but you must take the initiative.

- ✓ Seek out understanding.

- ✓ Do not let anger and other negative feelings fester. Yes, you can calm down, gain perspective, and then discuss, but do not let it go. Address it as soon as you are calm.

- ✓ Find new relationships that better fit you. If someone is "harmful" to you with their negative feelings, biases, and behavior, then seek friends who will be honest, but also there for you.

You may be unmarried and trying to seek the person to marry. You should test the pond. Don't go for the first fish you find. Date and have various relationships. If there is someone you wanted to ask out, do so because the only thing you are suffering is never trying.

Go for the opportunities because you may be surprised at the answer. Yes, a person may turn you down. The person has the right to do so, but instead of thinking you are unworthy, think that the person does not know what they are missing because you are a great catch. You are—for the right person.

Final Tips

- ✓ Wake up each day and decide what new opportunity you are going to pursue for that day.

- ✓ Make a goal you can attain for the day.
- ✓ Have a short-term goal for the week.
- ✓ Create a longer-term goal for the month and then the year.
- ✓ Have a record of the goals you have made, the opportunities gained, so you can keep your positivity.

Sometimes it may take longer than you wish to reach a goal. There are times when others are in your way, but you can also circumvent these roadblocks or move on to a new place or person. It will take time, there will be setbacks, but you can take opportunities.

Conclusion

"When you arise in the morning think of what a privilege it is to be alive, to think, to enjoy, to love."

– Marcus Aurelius

You are going to grab life's chances by the horns. You have steps to ignore the negative with an understanding that life is not fair or kind, and so you must act. Your actions need to build up with small goals until you reach the larger goals you have set.

Setbacks happen. Other people interfere and can retain control. But, what no one else can do is stop you from going after an opportunity and persisting until you have gained the opportunity. There are too many paths that can be taken to get what you want.

The best part is—you do not have to have a Machiavellian perspective—you do not have to be inhumane in your actions or commit illegal acts to go after opportunities. Instead, your pure heart, with enough grit, can take the opportunities you want—not what you deserve—what you are willing to earn.

Life is about earning the opportunities you want, through your sweat, tears, and sometimes your blood. You have the power, in yourself, to seek, to do, and to accomplish. The exercises and tips provided are just a short guide to help you get on the track you have always wanted to be on with the ability to succeed. Believe in yourself, take what is there, and at the end of the day, if you can live with your actions and be happy, you have reached the ultimate goal of life—to be comfortable and happy with what you have.

www.ingramcontent.com/pod-product-compliance
Lightning Source LLC
Chambersburg PA
CBHW031940170526
45157CB00008B/3259